DEFINITELY GETTING THERE

*The Fourth Plinth, Trafalgar Square,
Saturday 18 July 2009, from Crysse's
blog, Sunday 19 July 2009*

Tiger Argentina (limited edition hand-printed lino print)
by Laura Robertson. See p. 125, 'Tiger Dancing'.

Definitely Getting There

poems by
CRYSSE MORRISON

edited by HAZEL STEWART

THE HOBNOB PRESS

First published in the United Kingdom in 2022

by The Hobnob Press,
8 Lock Warehouse, Severn Road, Gloucester GL1 2GA
www.hobnobpress.co.uk

British Library Cataloguing in Publication Data
A catalogue record for this book is available from the British Library

ISBN 978-1-914407-45-1

Typeset in Adobe Garamond Pro 12/14 pt.
Typesetting and origination by John Chandler

Contents

Preface

Sometime in the late nineties, I stepped into a classroom at Frome College, where a diminutive figure with a magical presence commanded rapt attention from a roomful of wannabe writers.

Life would never be the same again.

I seized Crysse's tipsy acquiescence to take a cheap trip to Paris on a *Guardian* offer and the trend of two decades began; of travelling, writing, walking, drinking, writing… walking city streets together, exploring galleries and tourist spots, writing in cafes and bars across the UK, Europe – even one Christmas in New York (our indulgent Christmas lunch on a Boeing 747, having watched the sun rise over Paris on the first stage of our journey, may not have been Michelin starred, but we ate and drank with a relish worthy of a twelve course Christmas special).

There is something heady and precious about travelling with another human. Our trips seemed to caper through unprecedented magical synchronicities, and we shared our lives, loves, triumphs and disasters through our pages and our conversations across those decades.

Our last trip together was rescheduled through pandemic restrictions; a year later than planned, we headed to Teignmouth where Crysse's grandmother had lived when Crysse was a child, later her mother moved there, and previous chapters of Crysse's life unfolded against the tentative resurgence of a seaside resort post-lockdown.

I left Somerset, seeking new challenges – in particular, to streamline my portfolio employment strands to offer greater time and space to write my novel; in Crysse's own words, 'much as I missed you, I never felt parted from you. . . we stayed

connected at a creative and soul level. . . we both thrived as we maintained our steadfast friendship over the miles.'

The innovation of Zoom allowed us to pick up the collaborative work we had discontinued with geographical separation – we hadn't transposed to phone or email as ways of honouring our thread as an alternative to travelling together – and we were thrilled to bring out our push-me, pull-me *What's it like for you/Dance for those who'd rather not* with Phil Hewetson at Caldew Press.

This final collaboration has been a blessing (thank you, John Chandler) – truly bitter-sweet; exhilarating for both of us in the speed of its conception and birth (Crysse, I had no idea you had so much material I hadn't even *read!!!)* yet impossibly painful in our final parting.

You will live in my heart and soul, my treasured friend and writing partner, my fellow wordsprite, Live and Lippy-ite, Liquid Jam-er and playmate. Mentor and collaborator; your literary influence has been a wondrous gift in my writerly life.

My love always.

Hazel Stewart

Journey Request

I want to check in all my baggage, please.
Here's my infancy – birth trauma is in the side pocket,
those thin screams always go unheeded, no need
to tag them. Here's my teenage years – still in a strop!
This is my marriage, does it need a HEAVY label?
Too late for FRAGILE, you can hear when you shake it
how thoroughly it's smashed.
I've got a few other relationships
but I can manage those as carry-on.
This is the baggage I want to check in – just let me know
how much it all weighs, I'm ready to pay the excess.

Postcards from…

David Goodman

Gare Hill: Hurrying Man

Rooted
his gawky shoulders sealed
where wings should be,
his stripped stare
unseeing, unknowing.
He blunders on
hastening from birth to death,
afraid to fall,
afraid if he lingers
to have no life at all.

See photograph on the front cover

Dawlish Warren, Devon

February 2014 BBC news reported "devastating" weather in south-west England with homes in Dawlish evacuated and the total collapse of the sea wall under the main railway line.

Now as I was golden brown and straddling the rock pools
Along the laughing beach and singing as the sand was home
    The sky high and dazzling blue,
      Granny held me in her towel
    Wiping icecream from my salty face
And queen of the mermaids I wriggled away and ran back to the waves
Heedless of any call beyond their gentle surging swell,
      Toe-kicking the coarse wet sand
    All along the brown-sugar rim of the sea.

And after the thermos-and-sandwich tea, dried and cardiganed,
Princess was I of turreted sand-castles and splendid forts
    With scalloped moat and paper flags
      Flying their stripes and stars
    The whole world in my dominion.
And picnic packed and sandy shoes pulled on to go, we'd see
Slow foaming rivulets creep over our brave constructions
      Licking the ramparts into sandslides,
    slipping back into dunes as the sunset streamed.

Nothing I knew, in those childish times, that storms would obliterate
All of my memories in one raging night of terrible severance
    Rail from rock, rock from land,
      Nor that rousing from sleep
    I'd see the path to my past wiped away forever
And watch onscreen that timeless landscape ripped away.
Oh as I played along those Devon sands happy and unknowing
      Time held us all in ignorant thrall
    Believing ourselves as strong as the sea.

Tuscany reverie

In the thirteenth century
Castrio Castrani
though doubly dubbed depleted
brought sweet nut trees to these hills
changing the outline of Tuscany.

Here in Vallico as evening comes
cats slide mysteriously
into the distance
and the mountains purr in your arms

Storm in Crete

The sky opens like a blister, yelling as it peels.
Rain stalks the sea on staggering dark legs,
the sky forgets it is air, forgets
how to be air, becomes psychotic,
and instantly everywhere is made of water.
Canvas terrace roofs sag in seconds, become glissades,
the marble floors are pools, and red stains ooze
from the cliff edge as the bruised rocks bleed.
We stare from the bar doorway like children
watching drunken grownups: awed, speechless.
There are no words. They are lost in the torrent
that minutes ago was sky, and the word 'dry'
has been wiped from the world.

Transgressor

at Menelaus' castle, Kythira

I scratch the land for ancient relics
I don't know why.
The earth, vicious as geese
at the palace gate, guards its ruined history.
I snatch a stubby phallus from the stubborn grime,
once a jug handle. Now trove,
or rubble. Reality is porous here.
My legs are scissored from the frazzle of thorns
my backpack laden with crocks from this desolate hill.
I have stolen the past.
I don't know why.

Gümüşlük: Cat Goddess

I saw her on the Turkish hillside
swaying fast and loose on the sparse-grassed slope.
She was sand-gold too.
I'd seen it on the telly, that lithe fierce leaping
that's how I knew to be afraid.

I stopped. So instantly did she.
Synchronised immobility of brute mutual terror.
Seconds clicked like cicadas.
I stepped forward to screen my mounting panic
and she dropped like a golden rock to the saffron earth.

At length I dared to walk away, still staring warily
at my earth-coloured cat on the cat-coloured earth,
still watching my rock-shaped cat
among the cat-shaped rocks, still honouring
the obscure and treasured place where my cat lies.

Skyros: Visiting the grave of Rupert Brooke

'Here in Skyros,' the taxi driver told me
'We do not call this the grave of Rupert Brooke.
We say instead, we are visiting the Englishman.
εγγλέζος*, you understand? This is not
a burial ground to us. Stay here awhile
and you will see why he chose this place.
In April there are no noisy cicadas –
no noise at all, no sea wind or sound
from the rocks – all is silent. This is a place
between land and sky where you will hear
only your own breath.'
                              And I understand
it is true, as he says while he shows us the grove,
that a poet's voice did not die.

* sounds like "Inglāsuz"

Zakynthos: The last stage of mourning

All this week I've walked with a lion.
He arrived while I was seeking something else -
atonement, or peace of mind,
the meaning of life maybe -
not this mangey aged lion.

He's not the kind of lion I'd have chosen.
Flea-bitten and limping. Decrepit, in a word.
He pads beside me everywhere
quiet but determined.
What do you want? I say.

He looks at me through fly-caked eyes.
Butter my paws, he says. It's absurd – he'll never go
if I do that. Breathe, lion, I urge,
breathe deep, grow wings
and fly – you know you want to.

You first, says the lion. I sigh. I don't want to die.
Jump, then, I say – jump into the sea and swim away
You know you want to.
You first, says the lion again,
not sternly but stubbornly.

I take my lion to the beach. Surprisingly,
he's rather shy. He sits by me while I groom him.
I clean his sad eyes, cut the ticks
from his matted fur, comb him for hours.
He's purring now. I think I'll let him stay.

Cyprus: Agrotourism

At Pesterona museum the Cypriot guide
follows us around to talk of the war.
and I, ashamed to be English, stare
at insouciant faces in gilded cocoons.

What's the story? Here is St George
with long lance and disdainful gaze
slaying a small dragon. Making our history.
Blood streams like party poppers.

The slaughtered dragon crouches,
looking more bemused than fearsome.
no chance to stretch those stubby wings
 and fly, or even crawl away.

We turn to leave. The guide reminds us
these relics are from three centuries ago,
still worshipped in this Christian World.
I think it is time for a dragon sanctuary.

Liverpool Tate Gallery: Jacob meets the Angel

('Jacob and the Angel' by Jacob Epstein)

I didn't know what to expect – would you?
>An angel descending suddenly, heavily,
>wings like tombstones, dishevelled hair,

staring eyes. More like a gargoyle on acid
than a heavenly apparition.
He swung like a wrecking ball towards me,
clung to me, clouting my thigh,
>I almost fell, and he held me,
>his stony arms grasping, his huge legs
>buckled under me. I should have felt pain
>but I didn't. I felt sustained.
>It was what I had always wanted.
>Maimed, and claimed.

See photograph on the back cover

Devon Scrapbook

Somewhere back in time
a tiny girl examines the rock pools
searching for little crabs
and those shrimps that are transparent,
all eyes and whiskers.
She squats on the mollusced rock
fingers the pungent green seaweed
and dabbles her toes in the water rim
while the low-tide sea ebbs away.
Someone, perhaps her brother, sent by granny,
has given her an ice-cream. She licks
the dribble just before it falls.

This, the small girl thinks, must be
what happiness tastes like.

Freezing fog in Bath

Frost, crisp as cake icing,
tinsels the barbed wire into tiaras,
makes jewelled crowns from cow-parsley skulls

brittled beech leaves lie
on the white grass like a gaudy rug
swirling in turmeric and tan and flame

below the moon-white sky,
from the tall trees' high spires
fluttering leaves spiral slow-wale down

the white world is silent,
muffled in breathless air, the only sound
that faint crackle of feral frost relenting its ferocity.

Belfast Winter

Shuddering to bed in layered jumpers,
coats laid on top of blankets, our breath thick in the air
like a white gasp, teeth chattering through the night,
waking stiff and shivering.
Swabbing ice tumours with towels
from the bedroom window pane each day. They fall
like translucent scabs, like flakes of frozen scurf.
The fire eats coal. Only our chimney is warm.
Unwrapping and rewrapping my baby from night into day,
hugging him so the numbing cold can't grab him from me,
trekking bleak streets bowed against the bitter winds
and his thin wail. Spiky words blow my way like
the desultory hail: "That child's foundered, that's a cold cry!"
I know, you witch, we're all cold, we're all foundlings
in this grim city hacked from Siberian quarry slag,
I want to shout back, but the cold takes my voice away.
My toes are indigo, stretched like bubble gum,
my fingers white and pleated, my face rubbed raw
with cold, the bitter cold, the unrelenting cold.

I longed for those merciless days to end. How strange.
Baby days in Belfast are warm now in my dreams.

Gambia

In Tendaba pool
I swim lengths. My spirit guide
Is flying widths. Why?

London: First Time at 22 Betterton Street

Nervously
awaiting
my first metropolitan reading
at a laid-back poetry cafe
in a bohemian side street,
I ask the procedure.
"Just sign in when the guy
with the clipboard arrives."
Here he is
entering the door
disappearing under a scrum
of jostling poets.
Oh.
Is that how it's done
in the big city?
I grab a pen
stab a spot
scrawl my name.
Howl of protest from a bearded bard.
"I've been hear an hour," I bleat,
"I came from Somerset!"
"I came from hell" he growls.
I'm not used to sign-in rage,
I retreat,
but smugly.
When the readings start, the compere
tells us we have all behaved outrageously,
and all future readers will be selected by a lottery.
We all sit quietly
subdued but stubborn
with fingers crossed for a roll-over.

Puzzled

'She thinks she's the bee's knees but she's not,'
they chanted in the school yard, leaving her
wondering why, with wings to fly,
bees need knees.
After all these years, she muses still.
Not the bee's knees – so which part is she?
The sassy buzz… fuzzy golden body…
succulent mouth to guzzle stamens
drenched in nectar? She wants to be
the gauzy wings, translucent, fragile,
yet reaching dizzy heights, but thinks it more likely
she's only the bee's knees. Except that she's not.

Jolly Bundles

Howard Vause

Valentine Song

Winner of a BBC Valentine poem contest set by John Hegley, who gave extra points for including references to dog food, string, and potatoes.

It happened on Valentine's Day -
a good day for finding a frog
morose on the pond eating Chum like a dog,
puckering up for a kiss on the nog,
promising me he'd turn princely and stay.

The day after Valentine's Day,
poised on a lily pad watching the ripples,
penicle ardour our favourite tipples,
him plopping kisses all over my nipples,
the strings of my heart twang away.

Now it's no longer Valentine's Day
my prince treats me like an old spud,
scraped and then mashed up, feeling like mud.
I handed my heart to a warty old dud.
Now I wish he would just hop away.

Kythira

In Greece, nude bathing
is banned. But Aphrodite
obeys no man's law.

Bungee jumping crumblies

Look at them! It's obscene.
Wrinklies, tottering round Topshop!
They should act their age, not their fuck-me shoe size -
should be saving their pension, not prancing at parties
wanton and plastered, still trance-dancing,
still backpacking the golden road to summer lands.

Retiring? They don't know the meaning of the word -
refusing to age gracefully, won't go quiet
into that genteel twilight good night -
collecting tattoos instead of bus passes,
puckering sundried faces for kisses,
mutton-dressed brazen lambs, perpetual Peter Pans!
What do they think they're like?

This is what I think:
I'm not a sheep to be cut and devoured.
I'm not looking for a Never-Never land.
So don't confuse me with someone who wants
to be part of those fictions - why should I
change my life-long convictions?
Curiosity. Boldness. Lust for life.

Mirror Image

I watched him shaving,
slowly, tenderly,
carefully, round the lips
like a meditation
our hands together
touching the stubble.
I remember with love, but now he's gone
I think I'll grow my pubic hair again.

Where do longings go?

Are they biodegradable?
When you chuck them from the moving car of life
do they flutter like tissues, like fruit skin, and fall
into the hedgerows, catching on cow parsley,
dripping like dew into the earth?
       My longings are red plastic.
       They will not compost down.
       I see them from miles away,
still on the verge of the road, still stubbornly blazing.

Holiday conversation

I asked her why they separated
fearing tears, as you do.
She pondered, shrugging. 'I suppose..
it wasn't just the vibrator, dear,
It was that rubber thingammy - that
helps you open jars, you know -
once I had that, I couldn't think
of any use for him at all.

Planetary Forecast (in doggerel with germane bite)

I'm not being coy when I say, 'No presents, please,'
so don't think I'm churlish, or an irritating tease -
I love to browse the gift shop too, a real Aladdin's cavern
of bric-a-brac and gewgaws, and I nearly want to have 'em,
till I contemplate the fuel burned by the delivery truck,
which takes my mind back further, and then it runs amuck,
with thoughts of vast crates of curios criss-crossing land and seas
over thousands of miles, and I feel queasy unease
at the thought of the cultures exploited with low pay
to make ornamental knick-knacks, cash-crop for Euro-play,
all so you can wrap it up, and give it to me,
and I can say, 'How nice!' and pass it on to charity . . .
Never mind the packaging, these gifts *do* cost the earth,
and that's why I say, 'Thank you, but I've really got enough!'

My Evil Twin

My evil twin has no compassion.
Doesn't care how much she embarrasses me,
strutting forth, showing off,
letting people think she's me.
Laughing too loud in public places,
misremembering – mistaking –
missing the point
time after time
as if she doesn't damn well care.
I'd stop her, of course I would, but
she's glued my lips together,
she's smeared the mirror so I can't see myself
properly, and what's more
she's used all my own tears to do it.
      And then she's gone out dancing!
      Bitch.

A plea for combobulation

Discombobulated is a word with no return.
It means to **disconcert**, and that word flies solo too
as **concert** is pronounced <u>con</u>cert, and doesn't really soothe
it's a musical recital, and more likely to **disturb**
and even if performed adagio it still wouldn't **turb**
because that's another word we just don't have.

So what I want to know is, why can't I be **tressed**?
Distressed should have it's opposite, and so should **disdain**
If I can be **underwhelmed** and **overwhelmed**,
why can't I be simply **whelmed**?
Requests are **declined** and plans **deferred**
with no reversals for these negatives of life,
but if my plea is heard, and my suggestions **clined** and **ferred**,
How **appointed** I will be! **Persona Grata**, at long last.

Researching Nikolai Gogol

I giggled when I googled Gogol
though his life story is sad.
Gobbledygook seems cool for a kook
whose words were absurd and quite mad.

Sometimes

You see someone across a crowded room or street
and your pulse flutters, and your heart skips a beat
and you forget to breathe, as you stare.
You've never seen eyes quite that blue anywhere -
it must be sapphire - or such a smile. You move to meet,
your fingers press in slight frisson as you greet
and all you want is to caress, to closely press
till lips combine and bodies entwine
Because falling in love is like being spun in a tub of candy
        floss cliché
and we wouldn't want it any other way.

Life is Grimm but not Like Fairy Tales

You know it's a fairytale when the princess arouses
from a hundred years' coma as fresh as a daisy,
moist lips, taut breasts, and cherry nipples.
In real life each time you wake
your tits are more like chewing gum,
your peachiness more pruney -
I shall take no more naps.

You know it's a fairytale when the princess succumbs
to whines from a brute, and at her caress
he turns beautiful and pledges love.
In real life each time you offer your heart
he turns ugly and growls, 'This
is all your fault - you made me like this' -
I shall embrace no more beasts.

You know it's a fairytale when the phoenix arises,
the firebird returns, the ice splinter melts,
and the dancer with red shoes - *cuts off her feet?*
In my world there will be no such compliance,
no pragmatic submission,
no good conduct remission.
I shall paint my toes scarlet and dance like a harlot,
and when I'm too old to spin straw to gold
I shall start a sanctuary for dragons.

Review of *Pride and Prejudice* (in 26 words)

Artless beauty
clearly does endear
foppish gentleman,
honest indignation
jeopardises killer lust,
making nobility of pride,
querying riches,
sensuous tension under
veiled waywardness.
Xplosive! Yes. Zounds

Self-sufficiency

All she ever wanted was to find her feet
and they were right there, at the end of her legs,
all the time!

Senility, or putting on (Pam) airs

I've been having some senior moments
as down the next decade I hurtle.
Like, I used Wash 'n' Wax instead of Lenor,
now my towels are all shiny as turtles.

I've ordered all the wrong photos
though I can't imagine how -
instead of that wonderful wedding
I've got thirty-two views of a cow.

I have to leave crosswords unfinished,
and names keep escaping: who's Prime Minister?
Are we still in Europe? Who's heir to the throne?
This is getting a little bit sinister.

I can manage the shopping quite well, mind,
I write it all down on a list.
Then, when I'm safely back home, I find
it's my jacket and bag that I've missed.

If you're wondering why I'm telling you this
don't think that I'm crazy, or squiffy.
It's only a senior moment, dear.
I'll know who you are in a jiffy.

Onomatopoeia

I've always thought *celibate* an unattractive word.
It sounds like a fish. 'Battered celibate, please,
with a splash of salt and vinegar and a tub of mushy tease.'
Monogamy – what's that like, then? A bored game,
with no hotels. I've got a soft spot for *sleazy* –
it sounds silky and squeezy – but *promiscuous*
is a gorgeous word. Don't you agree? All made of
promises and kisses, and curious mystery.

Seasonal Renga

Spring
Wow. I never thought
you'd come again. You fill me
to the brim with joy.

Summer
I wait for these days,
they roll golden and endless
like fat butter pats.

Autumn
There's a charm they say
in gusty leaves. But I quake
with dread in your breeze.

Winter
My skin cracks, I break
inside, longing for oblivion.
You scoff at me.

Spring
Wow. I never thought
you'd come again. You fill me
to the brim with joy.

Oracle

I remember going in the bakery
with one and ninepence in my hand,
and the assistant said, 'Bread's gone up.
It's one and ten today.' I stared.
Gone up a *penny*! That's an egg –
that's half a pound of carrots. What to do?
We must have bread. And while I scowled
and scrabbled in my purse the woman said,
'It will be two shillings soon.' And I said,
'That's ridiculous. Nobody will buy it.'

Let us praise words!

Let us praise words that are fit for their purpose,
words like *floozy* and *scrabble* and *plop.*
Let us praise sibilants slithering like lizards
and clown-sounds like *eejit* and *Jiminy Cricket,*
shibboleths and oxymorons,
sweetheart words and swearwords,
innuendoes and prayer words, and insults like *nerd,*
and words like *isthmus* which are simply absurd.
Incomers like *Google* and *whatever!*
And let us not forget the fallen ones, interred
in tomes of etymology - words like *succuba*
and *florin* - we shall not speak their like again.
Invented, inverted, reclaimed, recalled,
let's revel in them all whatever their spelling.
What would we do without words? We've no way of telling.

Where do poems come from?

Where do poems hang out?
We go hunting them in the woods -
looking for words glittering in the trees
like sun-dazzle on newly-unfurled leaves
We stare into secretive dark water
eye-guddling for silver flakes of verse
or tiny words to catch like tiddlers in a jar
hurrying home, to watch them grow.
We watch the words as they congregate
we snatch at their swirling murmurations -
grabbing at fleeting images before they migrate
coax them to settle, so we can select -
but like scuttling wind-blown leaves,
like the wild wilful starlings, they entice
but they don't stay. The wind blows them away.

Another crone poem

Shakespeare had a word for it: OBLIVION, he said,
it's that last bit of living, when you're very nearly dead -
you're not sure where you are, or what you're supposed to do
and you know you once were someone, but you can't
remember who.

But that doesn't come at once, in stark capitulation,
it comes in swirls and clouds, like a starling murmuration:
some days you know your kids' names and your favourite
        quotation,
other days, your mind's on strike regarding information.

Next door's cat's name's at the ready, and the star of an old
        TV show
but that guy who's just said "Hi"? Your mind says, 'don't
        think so.
Memory files are on a break, data unavailable,
stall the man with chitchat, this conversation's not sustainable.'

I know it's unavoidable, it's a kind of natural curse,
a clear-out when the files are full - it really could be worse
and someone told me once that there's something you can do –
a vitamin that helps - I'd ask her which - if I could remember
        who. . .

Finding the right shade

The right shade of lipstick
is not too dark - not maroon that's aging.
Scarlet's just for tramps and wannabe vamps,
crimson is worse, the vagina-lip pout so blatant.
Candy? coquettish. Frosted far too fake,
glossy too slick, bronze doesn't suit my skin.
Puce? what are you thinking? Put it down.
Oh god. It's impossible to choose which
is exactly the right seductive shade
so as soon as he sees you again
he'll fold you in his arms and kiss you. . . and kiss you. . .
till he's snogged the whole lot off.

or

Experiential learning

I love wearing lipstick now,
not for the bold scarlet statement,
the cool touch or waxy taste,
not for the twirling glossy stick unfurling
or even the mirror mouth preening

but because
when I see my white tissue smeared
with a craquelure kiss
that red stain is never now my blood
just the mark of my happiness.

Three from the cynical card company

(1)

They say love can move glaciers,
cause hurricanes and storming,
shift the contours of the world,
or was that global warming?

(2)

You take my breath away.
I wish you'd give it back.
I need it more than you.
I'm having an asthma attack.

(3)

You're a breath of fresh air in my life,
but as it's winter that's a draught.
If you think I want to stand and shiver
you must be bloody daft.

That'll do

I want a man
who'll play Poohsticks with me
in summer rivers.
With our bodies.

Love, Actually…

Mike Grenville

Greek Islands

They seduce you utterly, shamelessly.
Almost banal in their obvious guiles:
the moonpale beach, DayGlo blue sea,
that ceramic smoothness of the sky,
slow swirls of mist in the ouzo glass,
warm air and laughter in the night.
And everywhere, like meshing spider webs
on thorny hills, a fragility of longing.

And there is always a moment
when reality and imagination fuse.
Amber resin of then, and next ...

I remember the first epiphany.
Burnished hillside, a priest
stroking a cat in the vine-leaf shade
of the monastery door.
Sun hacked the shadows.
Cicadas shrilled.
On his transistor the Beastie Boys played
you gotta fight for your right to party.

Greek islands are like that.
Virgin whores, sainted sluts.
Smells of jasmine and lust.

Winter Sun

Actually
it's not all it's cracked up to be,
going to hot places in English wintertime.
You come home, brown as a lizard,
baked as sun-cracked soil,
ochre as adobe huts,
bronze as succulent sun-filled sands

and you have to put your woollies on
so nobody sees.
Except your lover
who grabs your sunglow body
as you strip and doesn't seem to care,
as if he were colour-blind. Though later
he does listen to the sun-filled journey,
he does trace the contours of your baking,
just the way you want.

Local Honey

When she looked at him,
standing behind the counter in his black leather jacket,
she wanted to put her hand, quietly, on his
and feel his skin beneath her skin, pulsing,
ever so delicately, but she didn't.

When he looked at her,
in front of the counter, flushed with unaccustomed sun,
he wanted to throw all the customers out,
shut up the shop, and make love to her, there and then,
beside the jars of honey. So he did.

When he kissed her
she wanted to leave her friends, her work,
her land, her life, and simply live with him.

When she kissed him
he wanted to sabotage his reputation
and leave his wife. But he didn't.

How do I love thee?

Reluctantly, misgivingly.
Quite confused and knottedly.
Baggage-laden, warily.
A little bit besottedly.
Seriously and frivolously.
Excitedly and satedly.
Hopefully, playfully.
Curiously belatedly.
Increasingly wholeheartedly.
Missing you departedly.

word slut

We'd been to bed a couple of times
- once drunk, once sober -
but no way was I letting him
into my head. Then he phoned,
told me about this tower in Chicago,
above the indigo brilliance of the lake

and on the other side an infinite regression
of lights, as far as you can see,
all the way to the great plains.

I hate it when that happens. Words.
They get in your head, nuzzle down
to your heart. They glow,
all the way, into the darkness.

Villanelle for an engineer

Engineers have secret skills that others do not know
They are patient watchers, noting carefully each sign
Recognising how and where to touch to change the flow

They listen to the sound, they check where cables go
Then relax in enjoyment of soul music and red wine
Engineers have secret skills that others do not know

Engineers make their house a home that's elegant to show
They will reconstruct the bathroom to their personal design
Recognising how and where to touch to change the flow

Engineers are fit and strong, have energy and go
Hiking and cycling miles - when weather's fine
Engineers have secret skills that others do not know

Engineers are curious, they'll drive where others do not go
Then relax in enjoyment of sunshine and red wine
and their private, secret, skills that others do not know…
I recommend you find an engineer - you can't have mine.

Life skills lesson 1: how to fix a fuse

Obviously - don't let the fuse happen in the first place.
But if it does, there are several ways to try:

Seize the fizzing wires and ram them together, repeatedly
jamming their damaged ends, demanding they reconnect.
They won't reconnect.

Hide the frayed frazzled bits, cover them with a butter-dish
pretending it hasn't happened, carry on as normal.
That won't work either.

Stuff the whole thing in a cupboard, leave it there to moulder,
convince yourself it was rubbish from the start, chuck it in the
          refuse bin.
Does refusing to re-fuse have its own word? It's confusing.

Consider the etymology. Fusion means' Melting by heat' but
          also
'Union of different things: the state of being united or blended.'
Musicians and scientists treasure this precious process,
and understand the value of the fluid state.
Go back to your fuse and examine the damage - but don't bicker.

Consider how unknowably brief is life,
how weary is the outside world,
how precious is connection.
Candlelight is enchanting, and twilight too.
Hold. Hug. Love.

I want a man

I want a man who will message me all day
and far too late into the night
with preposterous protestations of passion
which I know, the second we meet, are true

I want a man who would walk through oceans
for me, and enter my arms all dripping wet,
who would whip up a meal for me if I was hungry
then kiss me so hard I wouldn't even eat it

A man who would stand in the driving rain to call me
if he couldn't get signal at home or his wife was listening
a man who loves cats, and jazz, and cool wine on hot nights
but loves me most of all.

Lover's Lament

Love barged into my life in muddy boots.
'You're not on the list, you can't come in,' I said
and Love just laughed, strode in anyway,
blundering through my pristine solitude,
stuck its feet under my table, chucked its socks
beneath my bed, left a ring around the bath
and didn't even care. I tell you, Love sucks.
Impudent as an alley cat, bold as a busker,
Love is a brazen thief. Stole from under my nose
my precious hoard of loneliness.

Scarlet Elf Caps at Great Elm

A half-concealed day, a morning between
milk light and grey, you and I alone
among the silent snowdrops,

It's almost a Romantic Chasm, this muddy path
beside the soundless water, rubble of the past
white lichen and dark ferns,

and we are monochrome too, unfurling
like pale moss fronds, and as persistent
waiting for a slow sun.

So what should we make of this sudden scattering
of scarlet fungi, tiny cups of yearning,
so blatant, and absurdly bold.

They may be dangerous, we say, still knowing
our clumsy touch could utterly crush
their frail audacity.

This is not a love poem

Because I'm not missing you, really,
not as much as I expected. I don't miss
your unexpected bouts of stubbornness
and perverse sudden deafness.
I don't miss those dire unfunnies
you insist are childlike humour. I do miss,
a little bit, your interest in small things,
your awe in nature, your voice, your laugh,
your touch, your foxy underarm smell.
Your farts in the night. I do miss these things.

See that?

He used to point things out to me.
Sometimes obvious things I'd already seen
 - a kestrel, a sunset,

sometimes more obscure: a bike
like one he'd owned, a house similar to some place
where we had once been.

'I can't tell where you're pointing,'
I'd say. He'd jab again, his arm blocking
my sight of the view

to stab at a cloud, or a numberplate
or a twisted distant tree, as if only his eyes knew
what to see.

I thought it irritating, not knowing
when he'd gone I would stare at an emptied horizon
missing the point.

How to relish a peach

It's easy, she told him. Look at it,
sniff it, caress its warm surface,
then taste the succulent flesh,
savouring the juice, the flavour.
That's the best part of a peach.

But he wanted to access the heart
of the peach. Which required more
than gaze, and inhalation,
That needed incision, a cut to the core
scraping curiously within,
while the soft abandoned flesh
curled, and darkened.

My Top Tips for after he's gone

The Dos:
Bounce back. Join a gym.
Buy solo meals and freeze your leftovers.

Find a face for the future. Use waterproof mascara.

Keep smiling. Watch sitcom repeats -
they're on all through the night.

Delete his number from your diary.
Erase his voice from your answering machine.

Change your routines. Avoid
places where couples laugh easily together.

Make some lists.

The Don'ts:
Go on long walks, hunched into solitude
like autumn stubble

Buy the flowers he chose for you,
arranging and rearranging their insouciant stems.

Play the CD he gave you,
over and over.

Argue in your head with him,
reconcile in your dreams with him.

Imagine hands, solid and warm,
dovetailing into yours – stare
at the full moon, fingering empty air,
as dusk bruises into darkness
and your hungry skin whines,
Are we nearly there yet?
And the answer is always *No.*

Postman's Call

You woke me up to show me the dawn,
garish pink as girly lipstick,
glitzy as spangled sandals,
spilling like Slush Puppie all over the sky,
and what's best of all, you did it
from forty miles away, long after we'd parted.

Ratting with Riesling

He doesn't drink wine often, I guess.
He finds two glasses in his cupboard
and we take them outside, where a yellow Yamaha
swelters among the zucchini, and an avocado tree
shades us from the hot Californian sky.
We're still in that time when strangeness
is stronger than intimacy.
My fingers smell of both of us.

His little dog yelps. 'She's found a rat,' he says
and he pulls off the metal sheet that leans
on the side of the shed so that she can pounce,
while still holding, in his other hand, his glass of Riesling.
The dog bounds, but the rat darts faster,
disappearing into the dark pine copse.
Of all my snapshot memories of our encounter
I think this one is my favourite.

Asking for a friend

And will we ever do ordinary things?
Visit the bottle bank with our empties,
squabble over maps and routes, know right away
and irritatingly where each other left our glasses,
eat a whole meal without putting down our forks
to twine fingers? Will we close the blinds
on the full moon sometimes, sleep through the night
like people do in ordinary life? And do we want to?

Charity Shop Shuffle

White boots sulk on the Oxfam shoe rack,
snubbing the elderly belts and bags which brag
their kinship of leather. The slippers are still grieving,
remembering, dimly, the fumbling of careworn feet
and a tartan blanket.

Cheap limey slingbacks, loose as undone bra straps,
make eyes at the nylon trews. Peep-toes, shocked,
mutter to each other about modern manners while
the tan court shoes fart, quietly, and pretend
it was the wellingtons.

Only the satin stilettos, red as touch-up lipstick,
watch the doors constantly, avidly, for rescue,
itching for the touch of skin, the feel
of flesh within them once more, the scent
of orchids and longing.

Dear All My Lovers

It's not you, it's not me.
It's that commitment thing.
Somehow all my careful boundary-stakes
flowering with sweet peas, bold beneath the blue sky,
turned into electric fences
twined around with barbed wire,
hurting us both.
I poured Roundup on our roots
when I said Yes to us, when I forgot
the cedar and the oak grow not in each other's shadow
and the dancing slowly stopped.

David Goodman

As Life Goes On

Proxy Botox

When every stupid woman in the western world
has paid for a needle to be stuck in her face
to poison her nerves so her expression is erased
of the subtle texturing of life that we call 'lines'

and that toxin has passed through the system
of each stupid woman and she's weed it all out
(and the lines are on her face again, deeper grooved
from the trauma of that unprovoked attack)

and the sewerage has been processed back into our taps,
does this mean with every sip of water,
I imbibe a molecule of Botox?
Does the unalterable logic of homeopathy decree
I too must look like a startled Cabbage Patch doll?

I have lived my life with human passion. I want my face
to show my heritage. Tears, and laughter, and all the long years
of struggle - my slow natural suicide. I don't want to erode
these tide-marks of my mortality. This is me.

A Couch Potato's Love Song

Gene Life-on-Mars Hunt, Gene Life-on-Mars Hunt,
strapping, back-slapping, you snarl and you grunt,
a flask at your hip and a sneer on your lip.
Oh, how I envy the gun in your grip!
You sweat like a horse and stand like a stallion.
You and whose army? You are the battalion!
Knee-jerker, berserker, your people skills stink.
You've no social graces, your style's from the sink -
but Gene Life-on-Mars Hunt, Gene Life-on-Mars Hunt,
nothing you do could cause me affront.
Foul-mouthed and hard-drinking, in fact mostly pissed,
my pock-marked Adonis, I love you like this.
The sound of the siren, the scent of the station,
that stained camel coat, all cause me elation.
Gene Life-on-Mars Hunt, no one could be keener
for a ride in the back of your ratty Cortina.
On the floor of my bedroom I picture your boxers
and you in my bed, passed out from intoxers.
Alas for my fantasy, dreams must unravel,
all for the want of a means to time-travel.

For those who preferred the follow-up series, Ashes to Ashes, use
the 'Gene Genius Hunt' version, and substitute here:
> The sound of the siren, the scent of the station,
> that slack-knotted tie, all cause me elation.
> Gene Genius Hunt, you're mean and you're rowdy what
> I'd give for a ride in your scarlet Audi.

For those who never fancied Gene Hunt, *WHAT'S WRONG WITH YOU?*

Feminista Not

When I was young, men used to ogle girls.
It was normal as rain. Staring on the street
– eyeing-up on the escalator – winking on the train,
wolf-whistles from scaffolding, lascivious leers at the local,
innuendo at the bus-stop – mostly non-vocal,
potential impropriety ever floating in the air
like Isadora Duncan's softly wafting scarves.

I used to like that.

Of course I realise now this was misogyny, and worse
– intolerable, institutionalised cultural abuse!
which I misinterpreted, through naive ignorance,
as the natural magic of human attraction,
affirming a promise of maturity to come.
I didn't realise, then, it was all oppressing me,
not flattering fun, just crude as a builder's blatant bum.

But I used to like it.

Million to One Chance

Just suppose I won the Lottery
and because I didn't tick the box for No Publicity
they came to tell me early on Sunday morning
in a white Outside Broadcast van
and knocked on the door
with the cameras ready
and the huge boom mike
and the big facsimile cheque
and massive smiles on everyone's faces
and questions at the ready

How do you feel?
Will it change your life?
and because it was Sunday morning
we were fucking
and we didn't hear the knock
or didn't care
and after a while
they put away their smiles
and packed the equipment back in the van
and drove away
perhaps forgetting the cardboard cheque.
They might leave that propped against the wall
outside, and the rain would mash it slowly to pulp
and wash all the zeros away.

It's late on Sunday morning.
That may have happened already.

This is what it means to be a wife

Your finger is circled in gold, like a magic spell
in a fairytale. Piing! Foreverness is yours,
now you are wed. Wedlock. Locked in
to your choice. You have chosen to be responsible
no longer to yourself but to someone else.
His happiness, his comfort, his moods, his self-esteem.
You must excuse him and groom him,
anticipate, negotiate, mediate, capitulate
and wear the ring that covers your skin
and shows the world the choice you made.
And when you stop being a wife,
slide off that golden circle, break the spell,
there is still a ring, faded and frail,
on the skin that used to be yours before
you were a wife. The cellular memory stays.
You can unlock the wedlock but each day you wake
your finger still wears that phantom ring.
You'll trace the place, touching it in the night
as if it were an acupuncture point for healing.

Sloughed

He calls me to look on the windowsill
where a spider cowers, spindly and translucent.
'Poor thing,' I say, and he explains, again,
as he has told me before, this spider did not suffer
or shudder fearfully. Spiders have this facility
to leave their outgrown husk - to slough it off.
He relishes the word as he reminds me.
I stare at the shrivelled fingers of that empty skin
crouching stubbornly, and though I understand
the husk is empty now, I say again 'poor thing'
as raindrops slide across the dark glass beyond.

The eternal reciprocity of tears

Yes I love him. I always will,
it's there in the dull edges of me,
it will curl up and die with me,
but never go. The other thing too,
that flame, I had that too, for years.
He nearly beat it out of me
but it survived. The space between us
fanned its furtive glow, and it burned again.
He saw it. He doused it.

Passion is never spent, passion is slaughtered.
My stubborn passion was hung drawn and quartered.

Why grieving is like a bruise

Because it's part of you, closer than a fingernail
            all made of dark blood

because it's something private now blatantly public
            and you're ashamed it shows

because it feels like a parasite nestling, violently
            under your skin

because you remember how it came
            and you can't believe it will ever go.

You said 'Can we stay friends, though?'

I said 'I don't think so,' as though I didn't already,
absolutely, know. I should have said
'We were never friends. We were strangers
who straggled somehow into loving
like fragments of fleece caught on wire,
or a yelp in the night which might be only
 a cry for help. And now we are strangers again.'
I should have said all this, but I was busy fidgeting
with the rest of my life, and you were already
looking around for the rest of yours. So I didn't.

But wild intoxication is not a way of life
and wailing for a demon lover is not
a comfortable part of our suburban strife.
And why should the ordinary be our goal?
It isn't mine. The bird of time
has such a little way to fly, and Lo!
we all know it's on the wing. I won't go quietly
through those twin gates of Sanity and Sobriety.
It's dark, it's late, it's probably raining.
Let's dance on the path to whatever needs reclaiming.

Misshapes

You told me you love me, you know I love you,
But we're misshapes really, aren't we. We don't fit
that heart-shaped mould with the tinsel trim.
I should have been your mother, cradling the child you were,
or else I wish you'd been my Dad, remote and melancholy
only less fearful, showing me what fathering means.
But we were born in the same time sphere
and we don't seem able to manage this contiguous journey.
I'll always love you. But I'm already watching you retreat
and for each step you take, I take a longer pace.
Soon all that defines us will be the empty space.

Plea

Will you look after me when I'm gaga, dear?
When I'm doolally, and roaming the streets
with my care-bear name-tag dangling from my wrist
incontinence pads, and lipstick, askew?
Will you come to my Home, which amazes me daily,
and take me out to buy an ice-cream? Will you
hold my hand patiently, and hide your grimace
as I ask you archly who you are, and try to flirt
with you, then, suddenly maudlin, tell you
your blue eyes remind me of my son who I have lost
and can't find. And will you hug me in my dreamtime
or will you tug me, teetering, back to now?

Ode to Autumn

I've hated you too long, old chum.
I'm tired of stamping on your derelict leaves
and dreading your dismal rain.
So put your weary arms around me
mutter under muffled breath.
I'll take your chilly fingers one by one
and try to thaw them into sweetness.
Sigh for me. Your ragged breath
stinks of death, but I'm faltering too
my longing lips sticky on that cold window pane.
We should be ready to forgive each other now.

The last tick box

Most men lead lives of quiet desperation,
My father used to say. He could quote
misanthropists at the drop of a tear.
Life is nasty, brutish, and short – another favourite,
except he'd sigh over 'short' and add, if you're lucky.
Gloomy epithets were his worry beads, or maybe
his lucky charms, fiddled with constantly,
adding new ones of his own devising. Sadness
is a luxury, he'd sigh, you're lucky if you're only sad.
Better for man to have never been born.
Snarling and pawing at life like a wounded bull
in a cruel arena, he lived into his belligerent nineties.

And his daughter? What of the little girl who listened
and learned, and longed to be hugged and held by a man
who believed those whom the gods loved die young
and despite his professed death-wish, feared hubris.
A strange quiet child who wished she was a changeling,
A recklessly miserable teenager, an unconfident mother,
Forties… fifties… And now I'm "65 and over".
After this there are no more tick boxes.

Final curtain twitching...

When you are a septuagenarian.
You have a new hobby: remembering and forgetting.

You remember when organic vegetables were just vegetables,
tomato skins weren't tough as polyester, and every apple was a
        Delicious

You forget the name of the nice person you're talking to,
who seems to know you quite well

You remember where you were the night Kennedy was shot
and the first time you heard a Bob Dylan song,
days when John and George rocked the world, but not the dates
        they died

You remember buying that Mary Quant dress in Carnaby Street -
When did second-hand became 'vintage' and cost more then new?

You remember when a ten shillings note gave you a night out
and the day in 1971 when all the money went decimal
(and that woman in the bus queue told her friend, 'It'll never
        catch on..')

You watch the sax player in the grey silk shirt
and remember you knew a man who wore one like that,
and you can remember the feel, the fingering touch, between the
        buttons,
the smell of his skin... But you can't remember which man that
        was.

You feel different from the people around you
but then, you always did, so that feels just the same.

Writing with a knife

You dip your fine quill pen in ink and write a poem,
shaping eloquent phrases with elegance and flair,
then watch your careful words evaporate and fade.

So seize the pen again and dip it deeper,
this time using last year's blood. Score the page
with wounds… then watch your gory words blotch and smear.

Wait for a while, breathing silently, then put down your pen
and find a blade. Now cut your poems with a knife,
your words not mere marks on paper but scraped from your life.

What Larkin said

David Goodman

Paternal Advice

'Don't blow your own trumpet,' my father said.
I was too young to understand metaphor (being two)
but quickly learned to mute that tiny fanfare,
bite my lip, top showing off, and hide behind
the polite and stifling mask of modesty.

And after half a century
of breathing quietly and trying to fit in
I realised what I should have said:
'Daddy, this trumpet was given me at birth
and if I don't blow it, who will?'

Trumpets and strumpets deserve to be heard.

Mother knows best

It's a stage she's going through,
her mother says, and she should know,
she's known her all her puny little life.
A difficult stage. Pestering,
tugging at skirts, whining for attention.
Whimpering for love.

She's been at that awkward stage for years,
gawky and fidgety, not fitting in,
copying that common talk and sloppy slang
just because she goes to school with them.
No need to ask to bring them home, start badgering
to buy comics and all that silly stuff -
she knows we're not like that.

It's tiresome but it's that stage she's at,
reading American trash, hunched alone
with rubbish on the radio,
storming off in a huff, out till all hours,
dancing with darkies, racketing round
on the back of that tearaway's motorbike.

Ungrateful, ungracious, treating the house
like a hotel, leaving on all the lights, wanting to marry
that scruffy student with his guitar, throwing away
the chances we gave her - it's clearly a stage.
What does she think she knows about love?

All her world is a stage. Her life is a stage
she's going through, since infancy,
gathering for her performance
the props she needs: isolation, loneliness,
they are songs to fill the silence.

In praise of boredom

When I was a child most of my time was grey
it was up to me to sift into gold.

While my parents were doing grown-up things –
my mother busy washing milk bottles, scrubbing potatoes
and fretting about the grocery bill, my father
off with his briefcase up to town, my brother doing homework
– probably Latin – I was fully occupied escaping boredom.

What a magical journey that was. Building palaces
from bits in the yard, creating dynasties from buttons,
dressing dolls in doilies, directing performances
with a cast of pipe-cleaners and matchbox dragons,
squatting with the big Encyclopaedia finding pictures
of Africa and Jupiter and places unimaginable.

I learned to imagine them. I learned to coax myself to sleep
with make-believe stories, and wake laughing with them.
Long before I saw a cinema I learned (that) my mind
could show movies – before I saw television I knew
there were magical worlds I could travel at will.

Now I'm sad for the children who never wander bored
picturing peacocks in the bare trees, who never fidget
ignored until they find how to unlock the torrent of
imaginings inside their own minds. I'm sorry for the exhausted
            parents
who no longer give themselves the right to say
Go and find something to do, I'm busy today.

Boredom and I parted long ago but we parted friends.
I'll never forget you. You showed me the worlds I live in now.

Dumb Insolence

'Who do you think you are?"
Well if you don't know that, why ask me?
my mute glare shouted back -
not a satisfactory retort, to either of us.
I wish I could have found a voice to say,
I am blood of your blood, skin of your skin
carer of your cares, wearer of your woes,
bearer of your baton in this diurnal relay
- or maybe I should have just replied
I think I am your daughter.

What my father told me about life

Life is not worth Living,
my father used to say -
not sometimes in a rage
but sadly, every day.
Not worth living was the phrase
I lived with from an early age.
A gentle ogre he was, shuddering
at man's inhumanity to man,
ordinary atrocities which
despite his erudite self-learning
he could not comprehend.
Better never to have been born
he said. Sadness is a luxury,
lucky, he said, to be merely sad,
but better to be dead.

Nice boys

What did you learn at your mother's knee?
Mine taught me
boys are much nicer than girls.
I believed her, of course,
she was the mother, she knew.
Girls are spiteful and catty, cruel and petty.
They squabble and sneak,
they disappoint their mothers.
They let them down. Boys are not like that.
Only a female could hurt like that.
I learnt it at her knee, that knee on which
my brother always sat.

Grandad's darkroom

In his dark and labyrinthine basement lair
my grandfather shuffled papers in magical elixir
and an image of me smiled slowly through.
This shadowy child was pulled out and pegged out
to drip, as the red eye of the safe light
glared from the corner, a secret deity
who must be obeyed. And I was proud to stay,
watchful, in the dark, with my sweet quiet grandfather
feeling obliquely, silently, beloved.

DNA

His father gave my son
his matter-of-fact manner, dogged slog,
egalitarian kindness, and blue eyes.
I gave my son
his love of walking and travel
and his residence on the road-movie of his life.
He gave my grand-daughter
her quirky sense of humour.
Her mother gave her
eye-catching beauty.
I gave her love of dancing
and total indifference to arithmetic.

War Baby

She was born in an air raid, knowing nothing,
reared like a kid goat, fed, tethered,
till she kicked off and found her own field.
She grew secretive and clumsy.
Always an outsider, she found reciprocity,
called that love, wed, sewn together
like two kittens in a sack for drowning,
doled out the same dark passion
to her babies, knowing no other way.
Scarred bruised bleeding, she clings now
to a fractured raft, not knowing on what sea
she has embarked, or why. Shallow breathing,
wanting to breathe deeply, wanting the deep,
not knowing why. Not knowing anything.

Inked

I remember wearing just my tattoo
baring it brazenly in the dimlit room.
He asked me what bird it's meant to be.
I don't know, I said, I think it looks a bit
like a heron. Wrong tail, he said. He knows birds.
I just liked the way it's totemic, I said.

I like my tattoo bird because it rises like a phoenix.
I like my tattoo bird because it's part of me now
I like my tattoo bird because I chose it, for me
not like a bruise or a slash or a scar or a scab
- a winged icon of me, my integrity,
inked into my cell structure indelibly.

Kind of Kerouac

David Goodman

Mistakes and sudden inspirations

It's a Kerouac line, but it whines like a Tom Waits lyric
laconic as Bukowski's urban scrawl. Errors and inspirations,
- I think sometimes they are the same. I could list
my mistakes and it would read like the litany of my life.
And every folly has brought me bliss. Every time I climb
a perilous crag instead of following route signs,
I find another hand outstretched. And the views...
How could I ever see these rainbows and sea falcons,
the distant misted mountains, blood-red moon
and awesome dawns, from that sedate, sensible, path
that leads without mistake from schooling until death?
I choose the clumsiness, the confusion, the impetuous risk.
I will get drunk at noon and dance at funerals, especially my own,
I will climb waterfalls and slide down torrents over boulders
I will collect my mistakes in a big scrap book and label it
MISTAKES AND INSPIRATIONS. And I will use an indelible pen.

Dreaming of my grown-up children

They are tiny and vulnerable in my dreams.
They do not smile. They cling fiercely,
the littlest in my arm, his brother gripping my hand,
The pavement is narrow. Fires flicker sullenly
as I steer them through the barricades of Belfast.
I pray the soldiers will let us walk on by,
will let us reach our lives, out there
beyond the flames, beyond the blame.

Gina Pane

Say it like Armani
think it like pain
obscene self-exposure
delusions of grandeur
was she seeking closure
or just savagely sane.

Why I did it

Doctors examining a 36-stone woman found an asthma inhaler
under her armpit, coins beneath her breasts, and a TV remote
control in her thighs.

— newspaper report

I am woman mountain. I swallow storms
like butterflies. Bees swarm in my eyes.
Below my arms are forests where gaudy parrots flit
through shifting shadows, between my breasts
languorous lagoons where dragons fly. My sweat
drowns oil slicks. Turtles crawl between my toes.
In my womb the tribes of lost children safely sing
while wounded soldiers blunder through the valleys of my
          thighs.
When I smile grim rocks sweat honey. When I shiver
the moon freezes. I munch the rolling years for fun.
I am woman mountain. I chew death like gum.

January song

Let us praise New Year resolutions, their pusillanimous
        tyranny,
and let's praise their abandonment halfway through January.
Let's eat more cake, and abridge that long debate
about detoxing, how much we don't need this big glass of
        Pinot -
would be just as happy without it! - oh, go on then, I'm not
        driving.
Let's admit this new year will be just like the last: a wrangle
with self-discipline which your more articulate decadence
        will win.
Let's praise the cliches and faux logic that let us off the hook:
'It is winter- be kind' - 'Men like love handles.'
Ah, the love handles of our lives, the soft slack self-indulgence
that underbellies every good intention. Let's praise bad
        intentions.
Take courage, take heart. A toast to whatever is hidden in the
        dark.

Is it time for Haiku Book Club? Here are your hai-clues.

Two rich single men!
Coquetry and confusion
but finally love

Gatsby loved Daisy
but the American Dream
became a nightmare

The valet is smart
But his master's a noodle
Therein lies the fun

In a posh chic clique
Being earnest is vital
so is a handbag!

*answers below

Yes, well…

        Early to bed early to rise!
        It may improve your baggy eyes
        but it won't get you the Nobel prize.

Trade descriptions

I'd never buy sex.
What if it wasn't
'as described'?
How would I take it back?

I want to write words

that are salient and succulent
and sassily succinct

that tell a tale as tall and gaudy
as Jack's beanstalk

that etch an image as vivid and indelible
as Edvard Munch's Scream

that smell like soft skin
and taste like ripe figs

that are pert and provocative as the 36 double-D on page 3
words you could leave on their own in a big city
and they would glow in the dark.

Blank page syndrome

If I wrote my poems on Ordnance Survey maps,
would they find their own way?
If I scribbled them on recipe books,
would they turn out saucy and simmering?
Would car manuals make them move less clunkily -
utility bills help them flow hot and cold -
would washing instructions keep their metre meticulous,
porn mags expose their soft and sensuous crevices,
prayer books elevate them? My poems are
written on blank paper. They gaze at me, bewildered,
not knowing what they are supposed to say.

Alphabetti Serendipity

I like: Avocado and African baobab,
Bathing in Candlelight, Dancing at dusk.
I like Empathy and embers, Firelight and friendship
and foxes and frivolity and fingering and. . . frost.
I like Geraniums and greenery and Grimms' grisly tales,
Heat-hazy horizons and Indigo-sea islands.
I like Jazz and Kissing and Lipstick and lust
and Mandolin music, and Merlot and musk.
I like Nebulous nights of not doing what I ought -
Opals, openness, Parcels and paradox.
I like Quirky quips and Rock 'n' roll and roses.
I like Satire and Tattoos and my ten toeses,
Unicorns and velvet and Voluptuous vulgarity,
Wit and wild words and Xtremes of ecstasy
and I like You, yes, you, and the Zing! of poetry.

Madabout words

I'm mad about words - I love to toss them out
like pearls for threading, cut and pin them -
cram them in a jar like Smarties, shake them, roll them
like marbles, whirl their kaleidoscope colours around,
spin them like tops. End-to-end them like dominoes,
pile them up like building blocks, flatten them like pastry
and pinch them into patties - fingerpaint with them,
fold the page into inkblots of splattered meaning.
Float them like ducks in the bath, chuck them
like Poohsticks in summer rivers.
Cry over their spilt milk. Dress them like dolls
in Sunday best, wipe their squeaky faces clean .
Whack them and wash them and push them through the mangle.
Leave them in the sun to dry. Press them like wild flowers,
loop them into daisy chains, chase them like butterflies,
swap them round like football cards.
Munch them like chocolate chip cookies. Tease them.
Push them off their trikes. Make them tremble.
Bury them in sand as the tide comes in. Bully them to tears,
stroke them in the night when nobody's there.
I'm mad about words. Join my crazy game tonight.

Things that are red

Some reds are funky and gorgeous:
generous smiles and crimson kisses,
sunsets that drop like a ketchup blob
through pimento-streaked skies.
Bulging peonies and juicy berries,
ruby roses in thrusting bunches
and goblets of New World wine.

Some reds are lewd and lecherous:
hibiscus blossom with poking tongues,
fuck-me stilettos and scarlet corsets,
vulgar graffiti scrawled on walls
swirling crude displays of red paint rage.
Glittery fingernails, flushed faces,
bodies' intimate soft places.

And there are mean reds too:
eyes meat-raw from crying,
plummy bruises and weeping wounds,
gashes from cuts and scars from the barbs
and the slaps of the past that won't fade,
and urban skies dark as old blood
soaked in the ochre of the city's unquiet night.

The Twelve Dates of Christmas

The first day we met
my lover gazed at me with
incipient lust

the next time we met
he asked me for a date with
tremulous yearning

the third time we met
my lover loaded me with
ardent compliments

on the fourth occasion
he brought me chocolates and
red roses

on our fifth meeting
he requested that we share
a golden shower

the sixth time we met
he brought me underwear and
a scarlet corset

the next time he came
and my lover gave to me
a necklace of pearls

our eighth meeting was
a theatre, meal, and feelies
in the taxi home

the ninth date we missed

he phoned me from the office
sounding rather pissed

on date number ten
we both had hangovers
and a row

by date eleven
the format was getting clear
rather like this renga

day twelve we parted
agreeing it had been fun.
I kept the corset.

Talking talking talking walking walking walking

When I was young I learned to walk and talk
I learnt it well. That's what I do.
Then life tried to teach me variations:
Shut up. Sit down. Be quiet. Stay still.
These graftings didn't take. I talk, I walk.
Life became insistent, gave me reasons
to be silent, to be immobile. I tried that.
I lived for years like freeze-dried coffee
dampened to the jar. Then I started to leak.
Drips became deluge, words became soliloquies
movements became journeys.
Now I'm back where I began.
Talking, walking. Talking and walking.
I must be nearly there.

Time being fluid

Words we etched yesterday
are ephemeral as sand.
Now is a gasp between *then*
and *next*, the misremembered touching
the unknowable, a slit to an abyss.

Time being momentous, now is ever,
Time being blameless, must I lie to be?

Time being flexible, will bend
and sway, side to side, as you dance,
will soften like a fig for munching
will glisten like gypsum in glassy rocks
will drizzle golden in your fingers.

Time being remorseless will suck you dry.

Tiger Dancing

In the forests of the night I called to my tiger
and he took me in his arms and now we dance.
Why is my inner spirit male? I don't know.
Why is my spirit wild, red in tooth and claw?
He needs to be. The rest of me's still a clumsy child,
anxious to please, ineptly unable. Cats, big cats too,
are savage and selfish and indifferent.
Now, in the forests of the night, flailing,
beneath a waning moon wailing,
singing in chains, scared and scarred
fire in my head and old with wandering,
my tiger dances me on, his big paws tight
but soft, his strong hold comforting.
through hollow lands and hilly lands we go,
my furry familiar, my fierce alter ego.

See Tiger Argentina artwork opposite the title page

After the Honeymoon

My house and I had a lovers' tiff last week.
I want you perfect, I said, that's all.
Just, stay as sweet as you are. Don't change
in any way, or age. It's not much to ask.

But my house soiled itself with spilled wine.
I wasn't angry. Just reproachful.
How could you? After all we promised each other.
My house was sullen, unrepentant.

For a week I stepped around the stain
blanking it ostentatiously. Then I relented.
Let's not go on like this, I told my house.
Life is for living. Carpets are for treading.

We all make mistakes - I'm sorry
I got so upset. I can live with your stain.
Too right, said my house, but quietly,
mollified. I think we are friends again.

Nevermore

You shouldn't get drunk, he says,
You know what you're like hungover. He is wrong.
I know what I'm like when I'm drunk. I'm wild and young,
I dance like a tiger in the dew-grass dawn -
that's why intoxication is one of my hobbies.
It's what I'm like hungover I forget.

I should be glad the curse is over, he says.
My woman curse. Again, he's wrong, I am.
My mother taught me when I caught myself redhanded
and called to her in panic: It's only the curse!
Then the bleeding cavern self-destructs.
You are yourself again. What self is that, then?

They've gone, he says, Just accept it.
The rocky world rolls on, requiring no consent from me.
Like a bird with a torn wing I understand my loss,
they've gone, but somewhere in my dark and messy mind
there's a pool of light where two little boys
like Winnie the Pooh will always be playing.

He says he will make me a cup of tea
because forgiveness is one of his hobbies.
He says the golden-brown serenity of companionship
is the solace of maturity. He is wrong. These wintry days
hot flushes are the best bit.

In the cusp of dawn

Tell me about the mistakes you've made
the ways you've stumbled, places grazed
windows smeared and doors unexplored, the eggs
that were smashed before they were hatched, the lies
you glued in a glittering mask of flame-red feathers,
telling the world you'd created a phoenix

Tell me the terrible tale again, the children you left
alone in the wood, no crumbs to make a homeward trail
in the milk-white moonlight of their dreams, whisper how
the golden eagle carried away your fledgling young,
count me the seeds you traded for beads
in the garden that grows only mildew on mud

Tell me your losses, list me your blunders
and blames, your precious offerings crushed
your dreams mislaid. Show me every relentless word -
words swollen in drowning, words swallowed in grief,

words flipped sunnyside-up while they were still raw.
Look into the mirror and tell me them all.

Not so silvery

As their thought hits the surface
my words scatter like startled chickens
lurking in shards of syllable
and when I snatch, they shatter
into tiny shards of obscure sound,
and the nouns - ah, the nouns -
first off the starting block,
leaving me groping,
bereaved, wondering how and why
this sudden exodus is happening.
Names flow away from me like flotsam
on dark water, unreachable,
and the meandering thought yawns,
indifferent to my agitation.
'I'm not going out today,'
it tells me. 'It's OK in here,
I'm comfy in these braincells.
I can't be doing with uttering - not today.'
You'll atrophy, I warn my words.
They burrow down uncaring.

Aspiration

Yesterday I applied to be a constellation.
They sent me a form. I needed a referee,
so I chose God, I thought he'd have some clout.
The questions were tedious and time-consuming.
Did I want to rise east or west? Summer or winter
visibility? Relationship to moon? (Cordial, I put).
Relationship to Pluto? Antagonistic, of course.
Would I mind sharing a locker with Orion, a parking space
with the Plough? Would I babysit the Milky Way once in a while?
I did my best, second-guessing when to say yes.
But Heaven is dealing with a backlog of requests,
though I believe my application is still on file.

Autumn Song

The town wears autumn like a toddler in a tantrum
fallen leaves flung everywhere, nuts hurling like hail
berries in bunches chucked in the gutter,
hedges and trees mottled burn-red and brown
garden blossom smashed - stems mashed,
last week's delicate petals bedraggled and trashed,
tiny trees twerking in a dance of violent disarray
and the mighty chestnut, leaves curled and cringing
lashing hopelessly against grime-grey sky.

Endpiece

My bossy lump

It's the teacher that's really angry, but says she's more sorry
        than sore
It's the lumped-up tea-cosy you made in Primary, and shoved
        in the back of the drawer
It's the thing you always said you'd never do, but did it
It's what happens when a good start all turns out fucking shit
It's closer than your next breath,
It's whispering all day of death
It's you, and it will kill you, as it hugs you like a secret sin,
Like your unborn womb twin, tugging at your pale skin.

*Crysse Morrison died on 6 December 2022 and was buried in the
Dissenters' Cemetery, Frome, on 19 December 2022.*

www.ingramcontent.com/pod-product-compliance
Lightning Source LLC
Chambersburg PA
CBHW050820090426
42737CB00022B/3460